# PART A

For the use of,
or on behalf of,
those with anxiety disorder

"Peace I leave with you;
my peace I give to you."

John 14:27

# Anxiety

Anxiety can be good.

You need to be keyed up before an exam, a job interview or performing in public to hit the top of your ability. If you are too laid back, the result can be lacklustre.

Anxiety becomes a disorder when the symptoms are out of proportion to the cause, and the resulting condition is disabling.

You may find yourself shaking uncontrollably. Your heart races, and you breathe too fast. You are afraid to go out because you fear others are watching to see you fail or make a fool of yourself. You are too tensed up to eat. You have panic attacks and are then afraid of another attack. You can't sleep.

When you are in the middle of anxiety, it can feel as if there is no way out. It can make you feel unworthy, a failure.

Take courage. Anxiety is an illness, just as much as a physical condition like anemia is an illness. There are things you can do to help yourself, and there are health care professionals who can treat you. You can find ways to cope and lead a normal life.

But it's still a frightening condition. This book explores ways to help.

# Prayers for *Anxiety*

FAY SAMPSON

NOVALIS

TWENTY-THIRD PUBLICATIONS

Cover design: Jeff McCall
Cover image: LilKar / Shutterstock.com
Layout: Audrey Wells

Published in Canada by Novalis

Publishing Office
1 Eglinton Avenue East, Suite 800
Toronto, Ontario, Canada
M4P 3A1

Head Office
4475 Frontenac Street
Montréal, Québec, Canada
H2H 2S2

www.novalis.ca

Cataloguing in Publication is available from Library and Archives Canada.

ISBN: 978-2-89688-746-0

We acknowledge the support of the Government of Canada.

Printed in Canada.

Published in the United States by
TWENTY-THIRD PUBLICATIONS
One Montauk Avenue, Suite 200
New London, CT 06320
(860) 437-3012 or (800) 321-0411
www.twentythirdpublications.com
ISBN: 978-1-62785-509-9

Originally published in the UK
in 2018 by
Darton, Longman and Todd Ltd
1 Spencer Court
140–142 Wandsworth High Street
London SW18 4JJ
ISBN: 978-0-232-53370-5



5 4 3 2 1 23 22 21 20 19

FSC www.fsc.org MIX Paper from responsible sources FSC® C103567

# *Table of Contents*

# *About This Book*

All of us experience a certain level of anxiety at some time. It can be useful in helping us rise to a challenging situation.

For some people, the fear goes far beyond what the situation requires. Instead of sharpening our responses, it becomes disabling. This is anxiety disorder.

It is more common than you might think. One in ten people will experience it at some point. It can have a serious effect on the lives of those affected, but take heart; there are things you can do to help.

In this book you will find information and advice about different aspects of the condition: causes, symptoms, managing the illness, treatment, how others can help. Each is accompanied by a prayer.

The book is divided into two sections. Part A is for, or on behalf of, those with anxiety disorder. Part B is for family, friends and the wider community.

I have used terms like "the one you love" and "they." You may wish to substitute a personal name or the pronoun "he" or "she."

## Christ the Healer,

You know how desperate I feel. My life is falling to pieces. I can't control my anxiety. The world has become a hostile place.

I feel so shut in, as though others are laughing at me and judging me. Comfort me with your presence and your loving arms.

I bless you that you reach out to take me by the hand. Assure me that this is not my failure – that I am genuinely ill.

I marvel at the Bible story that tells me I am uniquely precious in your sight. You love me and value me enough to die for me. Help me to take the first few faltering steps to begin to believe in myself again. Guide me out of the wilderness in which I find myself and back to a normal life.

# Panic Attacks

We have an in-built "fight or flight" reaction to danger. Hormones are released that make our hearts beat faster and our breathing quicken. Taken to extremes, this can develop into a panic attack. We feel faint. Our limbs turn to jelly. We either can't breathe or we hyperventilate.

Added to the fear that triggered this, we now fear we're going to die.

Understanding your anxiety can be part of the solution. Can you recognize situations that are likely to cause a panic attack? If so, you can prepare yourself by paying attention to breathing and relaxation.

But it may happen at random. It's common to have a panic attack when you are asleep. You wake up soaked with sweat and panting.

Tell yourself that panic attacks may be frightening, but they only last a short time – about five to 20 minutes, usually peaking after 10. This can seem like an eternity if you are afraid you are going to die, but tell yourself it *will* pass.

Once you have had a panic attack, you will be afraid of another one.

There are routines that can prepare you: breathing exercises, relaxation techniques.

It always helps to talk to someone.

## Christ, my help in danger,

I'm terrified. It doesn't matter that the terror has no real reason. I still feel as though I am going to die.

Take me by the hand. Let me feel your reassuring presence very close. Stay with me while the panicked minutes drag by. Assure me that they will end.

Lord, I'm afraid to sleep in case I wake up in a panic. May your comforting Spirit soothe me. Help me to remember those things that make me relax. Ease my tense muscles. Calm my breathing. Fill me with pleasant thoughts.

I need help. Guide me to people who will listen with understanding. Give me courage to seek my doctor's help.

It feels as if I am walking through the shadow of death. Walk beside me, precious Lord.

## Medication

If anxiety is disabling your life, you need to see your doctor. This is an illness that needs to be treated.

For many people, the best treatment is talk therapy. A trained therapist helps you understand the cause of your anxiety and how to manage it.

You may be prescribed medication, such as antidepressants, beta-blockers or tranquilizers. These provide temporary relief. They do not address the cause of your anxiety.

Antidepressants may help you feel calmer and more receptive to other treatment. Yet they can have side effects and even make you more anxious.

Beta-blockers can help physical symptoms like palpitations and shaking. They may help in particular stressful situations, like fear of flying.

Tranquilizers do what they say, but they carry the risk of addiction.

None of these drugs will get to the root of your anxiety, but they may give you help while you undergo other treatment.

You can ask your doctor about prescribing self-help resources, like exercise with a qualified trainer. You can follow up on many of these yourself.

## Christ my Healer,

I come to you sick in spirit. You don't need me to tell you how anxiety is disabling my life. Reach out your loving hand and guide me to where I can find help.

You know how my anxiety makes me feel unworthy, that it is somehow all my fault. Comfort me with your wisdom. Convince me that this is a genuine illness. Lead me to those who are qualified to offer healing.

Grant me patience as I wait for talk therapy to begin. Save me from sinking into despair that nothing can help.

May I accept the offer of medication but understand that this is not a cure. Accept my gratitude for the temporary relief it brings.

Give me the resolve to seek resources for self-help and the energy to cooperate with my own healing.

Loving Lord, it sometimes feels as though you are the only one who believes in me. Show me that others care, that together we can find a path out of my anxiety.

## Breathlessness and Breathing

Mind and body are not separate. A disturbance in the mind can produce bodily symptoms. The way we treat our body affects our mood.

A common symptom of anxiety is difficulty in breathing. This can be frightening. Your chest feels so constricted that you may think you are going to die. Or you may hyperventilate, when your breathing races out of control. This can lead to dizziness and higher blood pressure. Hyperventilating intensifies the feeling of panic that brought on the symptoms.

It helps to make a conscious effort to breathe deeply and slowly. This sends a message to your brain to relax. The increased oxygen will increase your sense of well-being.

Loosen any tight clothing. Get comfortable. Place your feet hip-width apart. Relax your shoulders. Draw your breaths from your diaphragm, not your chest. Breathe in through your nose. Let each breath out slowly through your mouth. You may start with a count of four. With practice, aim for seven counts in, eleven counts out. Your body will respond by relaxing further.

Practise this daily. You can do it standing, sitting or lying on your back.

Use this technique whenever you feel your anxiety mounting. And never underestimate the peace that comes through prayer.

## Holy Spirit, Breath of Life,

You know how panicked I feel when I can't catch my breath. If I felt anxious before, it's worse now. I think I'm going to faint. I may even die.

Breathe deeply inside me. Let me relax my anxious body into your care. Guide me to remember the techniques I've learned. Let me concentrate on deep, slow breathing. May I feel the peace that comes as my muscles begin to loosen and a sense of well-being creeps back into my mind.

Protecting Spirit, guard me against the fear of these attacks. Help me to deal with the deeper anxiety that brings them on.

Grant me the deep sense of peace that comes when I surrender my body into your hands.

# Heartbeat

Another common symptom of anxiety is a pounding heartbeat. This can be frightening, as if you weren't already anxious enough. You fear something is seriously wrong. You're afraid you are having a heart attack.

Ask your doctor to check that there is no physical problem with your heart. In all likelihood, this is a natural symptom of anxiety. If you can bring that under control, then the racing heartbeat will go away. Tell your doctor about this larger problem. You may be prescribed treatments to help.

Assure yourself that the pounding heartbeat may feel like a heart attack, but it isn't.

There are things you can do when you feel the symptoms coming on.

A racing heartbeat is often associated with difficulty breathing or with hyperventilation. Learning to breathe deeply and slowly can be a great help.

Your body will respond positively if you go for a walk. This helps to steady your pulse and your breathing.

It may help to call a friend for reassurance during an attack. You will be less frightened of being ill alone.

Panic attacks begin to subside naturally after 10 minutes or so. Tell yourself you only have to get through that amount of time.

## Lord of the Loving Heart,

You know how often my heart races out of control. I'm frightened there is something very wrong with me – that I'm going to die.

Place your steadying hand upon my shoulder. Talk to me in calm tones of common sense. Part of my brain knows that this is just a symptom of my anxiety. But my body doesn't feel like that.

Help me to take control of my body and mind. May your Spirit dwell within me, calming my fears. Remind me how to control my breathing. Let me feel my whole body relax under your reassurance. Strengthen my will to do everything I can to heal my anxiety and to do those things that will help me relax.

You have given me a life to lead and a service to do for you. Steady my heart that I may be a useful disciple of your kingdom.

Heal my fears and calm my anxious heart.

# Relaxation

Relaxation is the opposite of anxiety. When we are anxious, our muscles tense up, and our breathing and heartbeat quicken.

Body and mind are integrated parts of ourselves. Our mood affects our body; what we do with our body can change our mood.

Relaxation can be increased in many ways: mindfulness, meditation, yoga and, of course, prayer. You may attend a class, or practise your chosen technique on your own.

Choose a time and place where you won't be interrupted. Sit comfortably, with your feet on the floor and your back straight, or on your back on the floor. Close your eyes or focus on something in the distance.

First, contract your muscles. Start with your toes. Hold that position, then release it. Feel the difference? Tense as you take a deep breath in; relax as you let it out.

Move up your body, one set of muscles at a time. Make a note of any part that is harder to relax. Spend a little longer on this part. After you have reached your head muscles, relax your body completely.

Begin to move again gently. Don't rush it.

Stand up slowly. Can you feel the benefit?

Do this daily. When panic approaches, consciously relax your body.

## God of Peace,

You know how often the body you gave me gets out of control. I feel my muscles tensing. I break out in a sweat. I start to shake.

Surround me with your deep assurance that I am in your hands. Soothe my fears with the knowledge that there are things I can do for the symptoms that frighten me.

Grant me perseverance as I seek to harmonize my body and my thoughts. Convince me of the importance of setting time aside each day to practise relaxing. I give you thanks that I can feel the difference.

Be the voice of calm that speaks inside me when the world seems threatening. Give me the grace to recall how to relax.

Your Son could not do what he did for us without that daily encounter with you. Grant me the deeper peace that comes from sharing my difficulties with you. May I trust myself to let go into your loving arms.

## Talking

Most mental health conditions can be helped by sharing them. You may be afraid to talk about your anxiety in case people think less of you. If you do talk about it, you are likely to find that anxiety is commoner than you realize.

Friends and family can give you the reassurance that you lack. They may offer to accompany you in situations you find difficult. They may assure you that people care more about you than you thought. If your anxiety has a practical cause, they may suggest ways to deal with that cause.

If your anxiety is seriously disabling, you need professional talk therapy. Consult your doctor. You may have to wait a while for a referral, but for most people it's the best approach.

Remember, many people live with anxiety. If you join a group to talk about anxiety, you will be able to help other people as well as yourself. Just knowing that you are not the only one who experiences shaking, panic attacks and palpitations can be a help.

Talking about your anxiety is a way to bring it under control. Recording your symptoms in a notebook can also be helpful. It's easier to deal with something that is out in the open.

## Healing Christ, who sought out troubled people,

I bring my fearful self before you. My anxiety engulfs me, cutting me off from my friends and family. I fear that no one else can understand. Lift me out of that self-absorption. Give me the grace to take the love that is offered to me.

Comfort me with the knowledge that help is available. Give me the courage to confess my feelings to other people.

Show me the many others who are also living with anxiety. May I reach out and offer a listening ear to them and accept with thanks the support they give to me.

Thank you for the wisdom of professionals who spend their lives talking to people like me. I cannot cope with my anxiety alone. Lead me to someone who can help.

In the dark night that surrounds me, walk beside me and listen to my fears.

# Worry

It is typical of anxiety disorder that you can't get your mind off what is worrying you. Friends tell you that you are blowing things out of proportion. You should lighten up. But you can't.

You feel that things will get worse if you don't worry about them.

It can help to set aside a "worry time" each day – long before bedtime. Make a list of what worries you. Be honest: is your fear real or imaginary? If it's real, can you solve it? Write down practical things you could do. Then, if those worries overtake you at other times of day, tell yourself you will attend to them during your worry time.

Also, you can give your fretful mind something else to think about. Sort those clothes, books or photographs you have been meaning to get under control. Volunteer to help a charity with time, money or letter writing, and follow their work. Enjoy a hobby like gardening.

Make time for music, exercise and creative activity that helps you feel more peaceful.

Accept that you have stressful emotions. You worry about some things that may not happen. Understanding yourself can keep things in proportion.

## Christ, who bore the world's cares upon your shoulders,

Part of my mind knows that my worries are out of proportion. But I can't stop them chasing around my head, like a mouse looking for a hole to escape. I bring my helplessness and my anxiety to you.

Speak to me with the Spirit's calmness. Grant me courage to face up to those worries that have a real base. Shine your light of wisdom upon them. Help me to identify the steps I can take to improve things.

Give me the sense to sort out the fears that may never happen, and to decide what to do if they do happen.

Save me from worrying about my worrying.

You retreated to lonely places to see the way ahead more clearly and to draw on your Father's strength. Bless me as I set aside a time to think more clearly about what worries me. Give me permission to name my fears.

Loving Lord, may I always turn to you for strength.

# Sleep

Anxiety tends to make it difficult to sleep. Worries race around your mind and won't let you relax. Lack of sleep leaves you tired and less able to cope. The worries mount up. Now you worry about not being able to sleep.

Develop a routine. Choose a bedtime when you will be ready to sleep. Avoid bright screens beforehand. Avoid stimulating foods like caffeine, alcohol and sugar.

Use relaxation and breathing techniques to calm yourself. Exercise during the day. Hand yourself over to God in a bedtime prayer.

You may find that a sleep diary or app helps. Note when you sleep and for how long, the quality of your sleep, whether you had nightmares. What factors may contribute to your poor sleep? Understanding your sleep patterns is a step towards regaining control.

You may wake up at night, sweating, your heart racing. It's best to get up when this happens. Ignore your computer and phone. Have a snack. (Avoid stimulating foods.) Do some of your breathing and relaxation exercises. Make a note of this in your sleep diary. When you feel ready, go back to bed. Visualize something pleasant and let your body relax.

## Christ my Refuge,

You slept calmly in a fishing boat while the storm raged around you.

You know how I long for a good night's sleep. How I need it. It's not enough that my days are full of worry; my fears chase me endlessly through the night. I dread the thought that I won't be able to sleep.

Lay your calming hand upon my shoulder. Remind me of all the things that will slow my body and mind. May the breath of your Spirit help me to deepen and slow my own breathing. May the assurance of your love help me to relax each muscle. Let me get some distance from the things that distract and oppress me: my computer, my phone. Fill my mind with images of beauty and peace. May your comforting presence surround me.

When I wake in a panic, after too little sleep, may I know instantly that you are beside me. Your friends slept while you agonized in Gethsemane, but you will never leave me to bear this alone.

# Food and Drink

What we eat and drink affects our mood.

If we're anxious, it seems natural to seek relief in alcohol, something sweet or a cup of coffee. Sadly, these may make the condition worse.

Avoid sudden surges and dips in your blood sugar. High on the list of foods to avoid are caffeinated drinks, alcohol and sweet foods. If you can't go the whole day without one of these, consume it well before bedtime. Stay off processed food like sausages. Avoid additives.

Instead, eat foods that release their nutrients slowly: oats, whole grains, nuts and seeds. Choose whole-wheat bread.

However churned up you feel, don't miss breakfast. Try to eat small amounts often, rather than having a couple of large meals.

Some foods give positive help, such as those rich in vitamin B. Getting your five to 10 servings a day of fruit and vegetables is essential. Oily fish, like salmon or tuna, is another good choice. So are lean beef and fermented foods like yogurt and sauerkraut.

Plan your meals ahead. Keep the right sort of food in the house. Make a note of anything that stirs up your anxiety and avoid it in the future.

## Lord of Plentiful Generosity,

You know how often I feel so tense that I cannot eat. You understand why I reach for a glass of alcohol or sweets.

Give me a vision of my body as a house for the indwelling of your Spirit. Help me understand how what I eat and drink has a positive or negative effect on my mood.

I feel the world is against me. The last thing I want is to be hard on myself. I stand in awe of the discipline that drove you to fast in the wilderness. Give me a little of that courage to take my future into my own hands. May I do what I can to foster my own well-being.

You came back from the wilderness to enjoy food with friends and strangers. You were a popular guest at their tables. Please give me back the simple pleasure in good food – food that will calm my mood.

## Students

The impression is that students have a great time at university. Many do. But many others find university or college life difficult to cope with.

You're away from home for the first time. You've lost your support network. Others are making friends, partying and coping with the new work. You feel left out in the cold. You find university work a challenge. You're afraid you won't be able to keep up.

Your anxiety mounts. Faced with the demands, you feel sick and start to shake.

Hundreds of others feel as you do. The pressures of university life are real.

That's why there is a network of support. If you find it hard to cope, go to your professor, a campus counsellor or a chaplain. Talking about your problems is a good first step to managing them.

If academic work is stressful, take time to understand what you are taught. Go over your notes and your assignments. Highlight the things that you find difficult. Check things out with fellow students. Ask your professor for help.

Get regular exercise. Pay attention to your diet. Practise breathing and relaxation. Make a timetable that allows you enough time for study, relaxation and sleep.

## Shepherd of the Lost Sheep,

I really looked forward to going to university. Now I feel I'm out of my depth. I thought I would make friends, but I find myself in my room alone.

The teaching is different. I feel I've been thrown into the deep end. I'm afraid I'll sink.

Be the Lifeguard who grips me and tows me to safety. Calm my panic. Teach me to control my anxious body.

Nicodemus sought you out at night to talk to you. May I, too, learn how talking can help me manage. May I not be ashamed to seek the help that is offered.

You divided your time between solitary prayer and hectic activity. Help me manage my days. Let me give my studies the time they need, and not run away from difficulties. Give me back the joy of studying.

When I feel left out, give me the grace to look for someone else on the fringes. May I offer the hand of friendship that will help both of us.

## Exercise

There is a strong connection between our mind and body. Anxiety leads to many physical symptoms: nausea, dizziness, difficulty breathing and more. At the same time, what we do with our bodies affects our minds. The act of smiling makes us feel happier.

If you live with anxiety disorder, you can use the mind–body connection to improve your condition. Even playing with a worry ball in a stressful situation can help.

Better still, get regular exercise, preferably outdoors. It can be walking, running, cycling, tai chi – whatever you will most enjoy. You will come away feeling more refreshed and relaxed. Exercise helps you to eat and sleep better. It benefits your breathing.

Even if it's only 15 minutes indoors, build it into your day and stick to it. Try to do more on the weekend.

The early morning is the best time, but not the only one. Think about using your lunch break for a brisk walk and a picnic outdoors.

Physical exercise releases endorphins in the brain. These feel-good chemicals help you relax and sleep. Vigorous exercise has a beneficial effect for hours.

Regular exercise requires an effort of will. Choose a partner to exercise with to help keep you accountable.

## Christ who walked the hills of Palestine,

I place my anxious body in your hands. You know how often my heart and breathing seem out of control. I'm afraid I'll faint. Give me your assurance that there are ways to overcome this.

You understand how weak I am when it comes to exercise. You know I'll make excuses about lack of time and inclination. You were disciplined in your life so you could serve us. Strengthen my own will to make my body fit to serve you better. Let me feel the benefit in both body and mind.

So much about the world seems hostile. I bless you for the enjoyment that comes from activity in the fresh air. May I rejoice in the sun, the wind, even the rain. Let me feel my muscles growing stronger, my breathing deepening, my body relaxing healthfully.

As the feel-good chemicals are released in my tensed up body, so may your Spirit flow through my soul, bringing a deeper peace.

# Social Media

These days, we have so many ways to keep in touch with our friends, to share news and photos. But this freedom also carries risks.

Most young people care about being popular. They are afraid they won't measure up in looks or achievements. It's easy for a thoughtless or cruel person to post something that undermines that shaky confidence.

You may worry that you don't have as many "friends" on social media as other people. When you have posted or tweeted something, you keep checking for "likes" and responses. This can lead to feelings of anxiety. Stress increases with the size of your network.

Try taking your social media activity less seriously. Don't constantly fret about which photo to post or the best words to use. Give yourself only a minute or two to decide. Your friends likely won't treat you differently if you are less obsessive.

Social networking can become an addiction, affecting the brain like cocaine. Give yourself an occasional break. If you find you are constantly on your phone, day and night, put it away for a while. Concentrate instead on the world around you.

Social media can be good. Don't let it take over your life.

## Christ, my closest Friend,

People cheered when you rode into Jerusalem; they shouted "Crucify him!" when you stood before Pilate. May I know myself so securely loved by you that my life does not depend on the number of "friends" or "likes" I get.

I want to be popular. I don't have the strength to stand on my own. Surround me with your lasting friendship.

Grant me the compassion to understand that others feel like I do. Give me the grace to pay attention to others on the margins of popularity. May I encourage them and respond positively to their posts.

Take me away for times of respite, just as you withdrew from the crowds. Instill in me the discipline to mark out times free from social media. Help me to put away my phone. Open my eyes to your glorious world around me. Make me thankful to be alive in the here and now.

Give me the grace and humility to accept myself as I am. Allow me to forgive myself my imperfections.

# PART B

## For the use of family, friends and the wider community

# Support

Someone you care about is not coping well with life. They are not eating properly. They don't seem to be enjoying themselves. They look tired.

Talk to them. You may find that they are experiencing undue anxiety. Listen patiently. Take their anxiety seriously. Don't tell them there is no need for it. It is part of the disorder that the symptoms are out of proportion to the cause.

Do what you can to boost their self-esteem. They probably feel the world is hostile. Foster a genuine appreciation of their own worth.

There may be practical problems: pressure at work, money difficulties, a new or challenging situation. Encourage them to talk about this in confidence. You may be able to make some suggestions, but don't offer glib solutions. Allowing them to talk may help them cope with their anxiety.

If the condition is seriously disabling, suggest that they visit their doctor and a therapist. Talk therapy and medication can help.

## Friend of the Friendless,

I bring before you the one I care about. I know they are going through a dark night of anxiety. Reach out your loving arms to them. Use me to help.

Grant me the wisdom to listen more than I talk. Let their expression of their suffering be the beginning of their healing.

Give me the grace to take seriously the symptoms they tell me about: the sweating, the nausea, the panic attacks. Let me assure them that I am there for them, that I will support them with my presence when I can and always with my prayers.

You chose a despised tax collector to be your apostle. Let me raise the self-esteem of the one I care about. May I help them see themselves as you see them – uniquely valued and loved. Let me influence others to do the same.

Help me to find out all I can about ways to healing, or simply coping with these symptoms. Guide us both to those who can help them best.

# Friends

Social media can be a source of enjoyment and connectivity. We appreciate seeing the "likes" multiply for our posts, and the number of our "friends" and "followers" grow.

For others it may be the opposite. People post hurtful things, carelessly or deliberately. Few want to follow or befriend them. In our social media–oriented world, this can cause serious stress. That person feels devalued and unlikeable.

If someone you know shows signs of anxiety and there is no other obvious cause, bring up the subject of social media.

If this is the cause of their worry, take steps to help. Resolve to follow your friend's posts and express support. Encourage others to do the same. You may want to suggest things your friend could post about that will attract "likes." Cyber-bullying should be reported.

It's a delicate matter, but you may want to advise them to spend less time on social media. Anxiety can make people retreat into their shell, where their computer, tablet or phone is their only connection to the outside world.

Invite them out. Give them a good time. Be generous with your praise about their appearance and achievements.

Agree that you too will take a break from social media.

## Lord of the Lonely,

I bring to you my friend who is stressed by social media. You know it has left them feeling unworthy and unloved. Make me the good friend they need. Show me how I can support them, both online and in other ways.

May I use my influence to rally friends around them. Show us how to do everything we can to raise their self-esteem. Make us quick to counter anyone who posts hurtful things. Make us generous in our own responses.

Grant me the wisdom to help my friend find enjoyment in other ways. Guard us both against relying too much on social media. Help me to take a day off occasionally, and to strengthen my friend's resolve to do the same.

Anxiety strikes deep into the foundations of people's confidence. You know how to bring them inner peace. Watch over my friend and me. Grant us both the deep assurance that comes from knowing we are uniquely loved and precious.

# Work

Work provides a sense of identity. But there can be problems.

We may have a manager who undermines our confidence in our ability to do the job. We may be faced with new tasks and doubt our ability to cope. We may have a colleague who makes us feel uncomfortable.

If someone for whom you are responsible starts calling in sick, consider that the root cause may be psychological rather than physical. They may have anxiety disorder.

First, you need to realize that this is a genuine illness. Have a talk and see if anything is worrying them. Encourage them to report their symptoms to a doctor. If it helps, delegate this conversation to someone who is a sympathetic listener.

Review your work practices. Could there be any bullying or harassment that you need to stop? If people are assigned new tasks, are they given the training to cope?

You may be a colleague of the person in distress. Don't sit on the sidelines. Encourage them to talk about it. Respect their confidence. If you identify a problem at work, report it to someone who will help, if you can do this without compromising your friend.

Let them know they have your support.

## Compassionate Christ,

Give me the same heart of compassion for those who need my help.

Make me observant of the colleagues around me. May I be sensitive to absences and concerned about the cause. Let me find a way to offer sympathetic help.

Save me from thinking that mental illness is the fault of the person concerned. May I treat it as I would any other sickness.

May I do everything I can to make the workplace a source of satisfaction and creativity. Let me support those who find it difficult and try to make things smoother.

You called your disciples apart to refresh themselves from their labours. Show me when someone needs that respite.

If necessary, give me the courage to speak up in support of my friend. Open my eyes to harassment, bullying and undue pressure to perform. May I stand alongside a colleague who lives with anxiety, as you unfailingly stand by me.

# Children

Even children in primary school have anxiety. It is common among teens.

A frequent cause is the desire for popularity. Social media plays a big part. Many children feel they don't match up to those they deem more popular. They may even be the victims of cyber-bullying.

Exams or a new school may also create pressure. A different teacher can upset a comfortable routine. A child can feel lost in a larger crowd.

If a child is reluctant to go to school, if they are not eating much and seem miserable, you need to check what is wrong. They need a sympathetic ear. Assure them that anxiety is a common condition. It's not just them. Take their fears seriously. Telling them there is nothing to worry about is unlikely to help.

If the condition is serious and prevents them from getting on with their life, take them to a doctor. Medication may provide temporary relief while the underlying problem is sorted out. Talk therapy is one of the best forms of treatment, and many therapists often work with children.

Let the child always feel your loving care and pride in them.

## Loving Father,

I'm worried about my child. I want them to have a happy childhood, but it isn't happening. They're withdrawn and don't want to go out. They're not eating properly, and I don't think they're sleeping well.

Help me be the calm and loving parent they need. May I never forget to reassure them with a hug and a word of praise. Let me show them how much I love and value them. Let me not make unrealistic demands.

May I earn the trust that will let them talk to me. Let me take their fears seriously.

Give me wisdom to find words that will help. Show me where to learn more about anxiety and how to relieve it.

May they know that when I am troubled myself, I take my worries to you. Let me not be embarrassed to show how important you are to me. Yet save me from giving a false impression that faith is an easy answer.

Accompany us both through their fears and bring them peace.

# Caring

Living with someone with anxiety disorder can be wearing. You try to be encouraging, but you're met with negativity. Their fear of going into certain situations limits your own life.

Try to imagine yourself in their situation. Don't sound judgmental. Don't try to argue them out of it. Anxiety doesn't respond to logic.

Assure them that nobody expects perfection. Anxiety disorder has no easy answers, but some approaches can help. Read up on self-help resources. Encourage the one you love to do the same.

It's easier to shrug off advice from someone close to us. You may need to insist that they see a doctor. If necessary, accompany them for support. Make sure you know what the doctor advises.

Your own health is important, too. You need times when you get out and enjoy yourself. It may seem callous to leave the one you love behind, but it's important for both of you that you hang on to the vision of normality. This is what you want your loved one to achieve.

You need refreshment to carry on with the loving care you provide. You naturally feel responsible, but it's not all up to you.

## Caring Father,

I feel guilty about bringing my complaints to you when I'm not the one with anxiety disorder.

But it's getting me down. I feel as though my pockets are weighted with stones. I try to be reassuring, but it doesn't seem to work.

Give me strength enough for the two of us. May I understand their fears, even when they seem irrational. Show me the words of wisdom that will make a difference.

Help me to keep my own anxieties in check while I reassure the other that the world is not a hostile place.

Help me create a healthy lifestyle for both of us.

You knew how the pressure of the crowds weighed on your disciples. You saw to it that they had times of refreshment. In your tender mercy, give me permission to go out sometimes and enjoy myself.

Give us both the grace to forgive ourselves when we fall short.

Lead us together into the deep peace that lies in you.

# Church

We look around our congregation on a Sunday morning and think about certain people we need to pray for: the sick, those in hospital, the bereaved.

But not all illnesses and conditions are obvious. It is highly probable that some of those we worship with live with serious anxiety.

We need to learn about anxiety disorder. Knowing about it can make us sensitive to signs like unexplained absences. If someone seems more withdrawn and looks tired and strained, we need to follow up on that.

Any one of us can do this, but we can also report our concerns to the pastor and pastoral workers.

People who experience anxiety usually have lower self-esteem. Make a point of greeting those who seem to be retiring into the shadows. Tell them you are glad to see them.

If you are seriously worried, you may want to invite that person to meet you for coffee and a chat. Don't press too hard, but invite them to open up. Talking is a great help. You might confess some of your own fears and weaknesses to encourage sharing.

Pray for them, whether you name them in public or not.

## Father, who sees each nestling fall,

Deepen our concern for all who worship with us. May we look beyond physical illness and be aware how common mental health issues are.

Guide us to find out more about these issues so we recognize the signs. May those who have anxiety disorder know they belong to a caring community.

In your wisdom, show us how we can help. Talking can be a means of healing. Guide us to find the right person to listen. Show me if this is me.

May the warmth of our welcome surround everyone who comes through our doors. Make them feel uniquely valued, as they are in your sight.

Grant that our liturgies may be times of beauty and refreshment. Bless the people who lead those who experience anxiety to deepen the closeness they feel to their Father.

May we be a noticing church so that those in need find the opportunity to share their pain.

Keep us constant in prayer for those in need.

## Families

Anxiety disorder doesn't just affect the person with that condition. It's a strain for anyone who lives with them. There is constant tension. It's hard to plan a social life if one of the family is afraid to go out.

It can be particularly hard on children. They don't understand why their parent doesn't behave like the parents of other people. Worrying that their parent is ill can make children more demanding. They need to test that their parent can look after them.

It's hard on the partner, too. At the end of a day's work, it's natural to want to turn to each other for support, for laughter, for companionship, for sex. That's hardly possible with a continuously anxious partner. More of the family burden falls on one of you.

If you see this happening to your friends, offer help, not just to the person with anxiety. You might take the children out. Give them a worry-free fun time.

You could offer the partner a listening ear, so they can unload their frustrations and fears. If this is someone of the opposite sex, be careful not to get too involved. Perhaps ask a more appropriate person to do this.

## Christ our Brother,

You opened your arms and made us your family.

Embrace the family I bring to you in prayer. The anxiety of one hangs like a cloud over all of them.

I pray for the children, living in an atmosphere of strain and fear. Let me give them the reassurance of trust in you. May their own lives not fall victim to worry because of their parent's anxiety.

Show me how to lighten the tension and give them times of happiness.

I hold before you the partner of the one with anxiety. You know the constant stress they live under – how hard it is to remain loving and reassuring when nothing they do seems to help. Give them the support they need. Help me to make sure that they get a break.

May I be willing to step in and help my friend, both because they need it and to relieve those who live with them.

Make us a noticing people, so that families in difficulty never go unsupported.